My Own Damn Table

My Own Damn Table

Katie Simpson

Copyright

My Own Damn Table
© 2025 Katherine Simpson

For permissions requests, please contact:
Ember & Oak Consulting LLC
Montana

ISBN: 979-8-9931490-0-4
Cover design by: Katie Simpson
Printed in the United States of America
First Edition: 2025

Disclaimer

This is a work of memoir. It reflects my personal memories, interpretations, and experiences. While I have done my best to present these events truthfully as I recall them, memory is inherently subjective, and others may remember the same events differently.

Certain names, identifying details, and sequences of events have been changed or condensed to protect privacy. Any resemblance to actual persons, living or deceased, beyond those clearly acknowledged as such, is coincidental.

Some of the individuals described are no longer living. Their stories are included only as they intersect with my own lived experience. The intention of this book is not to harm reputations, but to share a survivor's perspective, resilience, and path toward healing.

Dedication

To my children,

You are the reason I survived, the reason I keep going, and the reason I believe in a love that never dies. My hope is that one day you will see me not through the stories told about me, but through my truth. No matter the distance, no matter the silence, you will always be at the center of my heart. And to the people who showed me kindness along the way, you may never know how much your words, your laughter, and your simple humanity saved me. Thank you for reminding me that even in the darkest places, there are lights that cannot be extinguished.

Acknowledgments

First and foremost, to my husband, Ken, thank you for being my safe place, my sounding board, and my fiercest supporter. You have kept me grounded when fear tried to carry me away and lifted me when I doubted myself. You have shown me what love looks like when it is steady, kind, funny, and strong. You are my home, my partner, and my best friend.

To the people who stood by me when life tried to tear me apart, your kindness was a lifeline. Whether it was a smile, a late-night conversation, or simply believing me when others did not, you gave me reasons to keep going. I will never forget that.

And finally, to every survivor who has walked through fire and lived to tell their story, this book is for you as well. May these words remind you that you are not alone, and that survival, healing, and hope are always possible.

Table of Contents

Preface

This is not the story I ever thought I would write. Honestly, I avoided it for years. Who wants to drag out their deepest wounds, line them up in neat little chapters, and hand them to the world with a smile? Not me.

But silence almost killed me.

It kept me trapped in an abusive home, an abusive marriage, and an abusive religion. It let other people tell my story for me, painting me as broken, damaged, or worse. Silence gave power to lies.

So I decided to break mine.

I wrote this book first for my children. You grew up hearing one version of me, a version twisted by people who never wanted the truth to come out. This is my version. My voice. My truth. Whether or not you accept it, I need you to know it exists.

I also wrote this book for anyone who has lived through abuse, betrayal, or gaslighting. For anyone who has been silenced, erased, or told they were crazy. You are not. You are not weak. And you are certainly not alone.

This is not a pretty story. It is raw. It is messy. At times, it is ugly. But it is also a story of survival, resilience, and rebuilding when the old life burns to the ground. It is about finding humor in impossible places. It is about learning that healing is not about returning to who you used to be; it is about becoming who you were always meant to be.

If you find pieces of yourself in these pages, take them. Know that survival is possible. Know that healing is messy but real. Know that starting over is not only allowed, it is powerful.

Life will never be perfect. But it is still worth living, fully, loudly, unapologetically.

Chapter 1: Life As I Knew It

Most kids grow up with safety nets, parents who love them, homes full of warmth and laughter, and families who have their back no matter what.

I didn't.

My parents were broken people who seemed hell-bent on breaking me, too. My mother worshiped my father like he was a god, blind to his lies, rage, and fists. She carried her own demons, abandonment, trauma, and insecurity, and she poured them into me as if I were her personal container. My father? He was violence in human form, with a gift for chaos that could curdle the air in a room before he even opened his mouth.

From the beginning, I was the scapegoat. Too sensitive. Too headstrong. Too much. My sister? She was the golden child, the sun. Me? I was the storm, blamed for the weather.

And we were poor, hide-from-the-bill-collectors poor. Dinner was potatoes for weeks straight, sometimes dyed purple to trick us into thinking variety was on the menu. Purple didn't change the taste. It just stained your fingers.

By the time I was four, I already knew I didn't belong. I remember standing in a cramped bathroom with my mom, the door rattling as my dad pounded on it, his voice like thunder splitting the air. My mom whispered for me to hide. Even then, my stomach clenched with a certainty most kids don't have words for: This isn't normal. This isn't love.

The only place I felt human was at my grandparents' house. My grandmother's kitchen smelled of cinnamon, cigarettes and Folgers coffee, the air always warm with something cooking. Soap operas murmured in the background, and she'd let me stay up late watching scary movies with a bowl of popcorn bigger than my head. She never called me "too sensitive." She just cared if I was happy. That house was the closest thing to safe I ever knew.

By the time my sister was born, I had already been cast as the outsider. She was celebrated; I was scolded. She was the pride, I was the problem. After hearing it enough, I started to believe it.

So while other girls were daydreaming about fairy-tale weddings and happily-ever-after, I was sketching out a different escape plan. Harvard, law school, a future where I never needed anyone.

I didn't get Harvard. I didn't get into law school. What I got was a temple wedding at nineteen, standing next to a man I barely knew, my heart pounding with one thought so sharp it cut through the veil. This is the biggest mistake of my life.

And I was right. But what I couldn't have known then was that the greatest mistake of my life would lead me to its greatest love.

Chapter 2: Greatest Love

The best thing I've ever done in my life is having kids. Hands down. They were my lifeline, my reason to keep breathing when everything else around me screamed, *Give Up*.

My first daughter came into the world in 1995, three weeks early and already determined to do things her own way. She was tiny, perfect, and mine. I remember holding her for the first time, her cheek soft against my skin, and thinking: This is it. This is the reason I'm alive. For the first time in my life, love wasn't conditional, manipulative, or twisted. It was just... love.

My husband at the time couldn't have cared less. His world revolved around cars, tools, and himself; family was barely a footnote. Helping me? That was beneath him. I learned quickly that motherhood wasn't going to be a partnership. Fine. I was built for survival.

In 1997, my son arrived, quiet, serious, an old soul from the start. He crawled at five months and seemed to study the world like he already knew more than the rest of us. But life wasn't easy for him. Chronic ear infections meant surgeries, speech therapy, and endless nights of worry. Feeding him nearly broke me. I ended up with mastitis so severe that I wasn't sure I'd make it through. My husband's response? Still checked out. His idea of "support" was parking himself in the garage with his latest tool.

Then came my third child, another son, in 1998. He was premature, and I spent three long weeks in the hospital before he was born. Fragile, struggling to breathe, yet full of light. He had this smile that seemed to take up his whole face, as if joy was his first language. He was late to talk, and when I asked the doctor if something was wrong, the response was, "He doesn't need to talk; his siblings do it for him." Honestly, that's probably still true.

Finally, in 2001, my youngest daughter arrived five weeks early. She was sunshine in the middle of a storm I couldn't control, radiant, kind, deeply connected to me. By then, my marriage was already crumbling around me, but every time I looked at her, I was reminded that good still existed in the world.

The truth is, motherhood was the greatest love I'd ever known, but it was also the greatest heartbreak. Because while I poured everything I had into raising my children, their father was busy tearing it all apart.

There were nights I believed my life could end in an instant, when he pressed a gun to my head and told me he held the power to erase me whenever he wanted. Days when he hit me because I dared to "not listen." Once, he dragged me naked out of the shower, screaming that I needed to be punished. I remember climbing back under the water afterward, shaking, sobbing, begging God to get me out. But sometimes the bruises weren't on my body—they were in my heart. He withheld affection, treated me like I was disposable, and made sure I knew I didn't matter. The words cut as deeply as the fists. You're nothing. You'll never be enough. No one will ever want you. Those echoes lived inside me long after the bruises faded, convincing me for years that I was unworthy of even the most basic love.

But the worst wasn't what he did to me. It was what he did to them. I'll never forget the day in the car when he turned and punched my oldest son in the face unprovoked. The kids cried out in the backseat, terror sharp in their voices. My hands shook as I slammed the car to the side of the road, told him to get the hell out, and drove away. That was the day I knew I had to leave. Not for me. For them.

Motherhood gave me the courage I couldn't find anywhere else. My children were the reason I endured as long as I did, and the reason I finally walked away.

They were, and always will be, my greatest love.

Chapter 3: Expectations (and Explosions)

I left my marriage on Valentine's Day.

Some women get roses, chocolates, and candlelight. I got a borrowed truck, two friends willing to risk my husband's wrath, and a thirty-minute window to grab what I could before he showed up. Honestly, it felt more romantic than anything he had ever given me.

Ten years of marriage, and not once had he celebrated a holiday, my birthday, or anything that mattered to me. Not once. Instead, he reminded me daily that I wasn't worthy of his love. His favorite refrain? That he had "let the love of his life" slip away, and I would never measure up. Imagine hearing that on repeat, and still being expected to clean the house, cook dinner, and smile like you were the lucky one.

So yes, leaving on Valentine's Day felt fitting, my parting gift to myself.

At first, I thought maybe things would settle. The kids weren't sad about leaving; they were relieved. Excited, even. That told me everything I needed to know. I had worried for so long about "breaking up the family," but the truth was, there hadn't been a family to break in years. Just a house held together by fear.

But my husband wasn't about to let go of control. He came to my door begging, threatening, switching masks like a man auditioning for every role in the same play: the sad, wounded victim; the raging tyrant; the desperate charmer. When none of it worked, he did what narcissists do best: he went to war.

He hired an attorney, the very same one I had once used. That man should have recused himself, but of course, he didn't. In a small town, corruption isn't a scandal; it's tradition. Suddenly, I wasn't just facing my abusive ex. I was staring down a legal system that had already decided whose side it was on.

I filed motion after motion to have that attorney removed. Every attempt failed. Instead, the two of them joined forces in a smear campaign designed to destroy me. My ex spun himself as the poor, abandoned husband. Church leaders, family members, and mutual friends lined up to nod along.

It was classic narcissism: projection, manipulation, a flawless performance for the audience while the cruelty raged behind closed doors. At the time, though, I didn't have the word for it. I just thought I was losing my mind.

The late-night phone calls were the worst. His voice dripping with venom: "Are you ready to end it all? I know you have a gun. Because if you're not, I'll see to it." He promised I'd never get the kids. Promised he'd destroy me. And he bragged, actually bragged, about turning my family and friends against me. The part that gutted me most was knowing he wasn't lying.

Meanwhile, the kids were stuck in the middle of his theater. At his house, they weren't even allowed to say my name. If they slipped and called me "Mom," they were punished. Piece by piece, he was erasing me from their lives.

And as if that wasn't enough, he moved on, straight into the arms of a married woman who had once been my closest friend. Together, they made it their mission to ruin me. If I ever doubted that cruelty could find a soulmate, that relationship proved me wrong.

Then came the night everything shifted.

It was August, one of those suffocating evenings when the air feels heavy enough to crush you. The kids and I were in our rental, trying to settle in for bed, when the basement door slammed open. A voice shouted threats to kill us. Shadows moved past the windows. Footsteps circled the house. The kids sobbed, clinging to me, while my pulse hammered so hard I thought it might rip through my chest.

I wanted to call the police. But I knew better. My ex was friends with the sheriff. He'd already poisoned the well, convincing them I was a liar. The domestic violence advocates were told not to help me. I wasn't just unprotected, I was targeted.

So I did the only thing left. I sat in my bedroom doorway with a loaded handgun across my lap, my children asleep in my bed behind me, and I made a promise: if anyone came through that door, I was going to pull the trigger.

That night, the truth crystallized. If I stayed, I would die. And worse, my children would be left with him, believing his lies about me.

I didn't just need to leave the marriage. I had to leave the town. The house. The life I'd known.

Everything.

Chapter 4: The Knowing

There comes a point when you stop debating with yourself. The fear, the what-ifs, the guilt, they all get drowned out by a single, bone-deep truth: If I don't leave, I won't survive.

That was me.

By then, two truths were carved into my soul:

If I stayed in that town with him, I'd end up dead, and they'd make sure it looked like an accident.

If I left, I would leave without my children.

No mother should ever have to make that choice. But there I was, alone, cornered by a corrupt legal system, a church that protected abusers, and a family who cheered on my destruction.

It wasn't fear anymore. It was certainty.

I had already survived death threats, beatings, and a legal circus stacked against me. I had lived through the August break-in, sitting in my doorway with a loaded gun across my lap while my babies slept in my bed. I knew no one was coming to save me. If anything, the sheriff would have handed the intruder a flashlight.

So I did what survivors do; I made a plan.

In five days, I drove over a thousand miles, scouted a new town, landed a job with full benefits, and found a place to live. Call it desperation, call it divine intervention, but when your life is on the line, you don't waste time. Then I went back, packed my determination like armor, and waited for the right moment.

That moment came during a custody hearing. I knew before I walked in that I was going to lose. Everyone in that courtroom had already decided who I was: the unstable wife, the unfit mother. My husband's smear campaign had worked. The church leaders backed him. My family testified against me. I didn't stand a chance.

What they didn't know was that while I sat there being stripped of custody and visitation, a moving truck was already on the highway with everything I owned. By the time the judge's gavel fell, my life was already gone from that town.

As I drove away, my phone rang. It was the church bishop. Smug as ever, he informed me he'd been at the hearing and that I was going to be excommunicated.

I gripped the steering wheel tighter, pressed down on the gas, and said, "You can fuck right off." Then I hung up.

And then it happened.

Clear as day, a voice filled the car. Not outside. Not imagined. Inside me.

"It's going to get bad. Really bad. But you'll be okay. It will all work out in the end."

For the first time in years, I believed it.

That knowing wasn't fear. It wasn't instinct. It was guidance. The universe, God, my higher self, call it whatever you want. It was real. And it told me to keep driving.

So I did. Away from the church. Away from the abuse. Away from the ashes of a life that had never truly been mine.

I didn't know what the future held. But I knew one thing for certain. I was finally free to find out.

Chapter 5: Coming to Terms

When I left without my children, I believed I had committed the ultimate betrayal. For years, that guilt strapped itself to my back like a boulder I couldn't shake. Every night, it whispered the same poison: What kind of mother leaves her kids?

But here's the truth no one wants to say out loud: sometimes survival looks like failure from the outside. Staying would have killed me. And dead mothers don't win custody battles. Dead mothers don't tell their stories.

So instead of letting the guilt crush me, I made a deal with myself. If I couldn't be with my children, then every single thing I did from that day forward would be for them. Every decision, every risk, every ounce of fight, it would all be about building a life worth showing them someday.

And guilt, as brutal as it was, became fuel.

I worked harder than I ever thought possible. I clawed my way out of nothing: no support system, no family, no church, no children. Every morning I woke up without them, I pushed harder. Every night I went to bed missing them, I promised myself I would carve something meaningful out of the wreckage.

But it wasn't just about survival. It was about identity. About finally coming to terms with who I was, and who I wasn't.

I wasn't the unstable woman my ex painted me to be. I wasn't the scapegoat my family claimed I was. And I damn sure wasn't the sinner the church tried to brand me as.

I was a mother. A fighter. A woman who had stopped begging for scraps of love and decided to build her own damn table.

Did it hurt? Absolutely. There were nights I cried until my chest ached and my eyes burned. Nights when silence filled the house so thick it felt suffocating. Nights when I replayed every custody hearing, every betrayal, every lie my children were taught to believe about me.

But here's the thing: pain offers two choices. It can bury you, or it can build you. I decided mine was going to build me.

So I learned to sit with it. To accept that regret would always sting, but it didn't have to define me. I stopped asking, Why me? and started asking, Now what?

Coming to terms with my losses didn't mean surrender. It meant turning grief into grit. It meant refusing to let my abuser, my family, or my church write the ending of my story.

And it meant holding on to one stubborn, unshakable truth: one day, my kids would know who I really was.

Until then, I would live in a way that made me proud of the woman they would eventually see.

Chapter 6: Making Bold Moves

When you've been torn down your whole life, by parents, by a spouse, by a church, by an entire system, there comes a point when you stop waiting for permission.

That was me.

For years, I lived with the same broken soundtrack playing on repeat. You're worthless. You're stupid. You'll never make it on your own. My father once bragged that I was the only kid dumb enough to come back from college "stupider" than when I left. My mother sighed in disappointment if it was her native tongue. The church branded me a sinner. My ex called me crazy.

Fine. If that's who they thought I was, then proving them wrong became my mission.

So I started making bold moves.

First, I threw myself into work. No family to lean on. No safety net. No backup plan. Just me, a paycheck, and sheer stubbornness. Independence might not have been glamorous, but it tasted better than any sacrament bread I'd ever been handed.

I bought my own car. Paid my own bills. Went back to school on my own terms. For the first time in my life, nobody else was pulling the strings, except me.

And then I began unlearning the programming that had chained me for so long.

The church had promised that if I played the role, show up every Sunday, pay tithing, obey without question, God would bless me. What did that get me? An abusive husband, a corrupt bishop, and a courtroom weaponized against me. So I stopped believing in their God, the one who looked a lot like my father and my ex: punishing, controlling, always right.

Instead, I started believing in myself. In my instincts. In that quiet, steady knowing I'd heard the day I drove out of town: *It's going to get bad. But you'll be okay.*

That didn't erase the scars. The memories still lingered, sharp, unhealed wounds I carried everywhere. Like senior prom, when I was crowned queen on the biggest night of my teenage life. And yet, I was the only girl in the room whose parents didn't bother to show up for a single photograph. Or the scholarships and awards I clawed my way to earn, only to be told they meant nothing because I was still nothing. Still a disappointment.

Those memories haunted me. But they also fueled me. Every time I replayed my family's cruelty, I pushed harder. Every time their voices crept into my head, I drowned them out with my own: You will not win. I will.

The nightmares followed me, too. One etched itself into my soul: I was standing outside my family's home, lining up for a photograph. Then someone told me to step back and take the picture instead. I lifted the camera, looked through the lens, and saw them, my parents, my sister, my husband, all smiling together. And behind them stood the devil himself, arms draped around them, leering straight at me. I woke up screaming.

It wasn't just a dream. It was a message. My family had never truly been mine. Their loyalty had always been spoken for, and it was never with me.

So I stopped begging for scraps of their love. I stopped chasing approval that was never going to be given.

And instead, I started making bold moves for myself. For my future. For the life I was determined to claim.

Little by little, the truth revealed itself: I wasn't weak. I wasn't worthless. I wasn't crazy.

I was powerful.

And I was just getting started.

Chapter 7: Teenage Years: The Shattering

Most kids remember high school as a blur of football games, dances, and awkward teenage crushes. I had those moments too, late nights at the park with friends, pretending not to watch boys play basketball, getting ready for dances, wondering if my hair was big enough. On the surface, I looked like any other teenage girl.

But beneath that surface, my world was brutal.

When I was fifteen, my father showed up at the park where I was hanging out with friends. One moment I was laughing, and the next his hand clamped down on my arm so hard I thought he might rip it out of the socket. In front of everyone, he sneered that I was acting like a "dog in heat." The shame of that moment carved so deep it rewired something in me. It shattered my confidence and left a scar on my self-worth that I carried for decades.

And it didn't stop there.

At sixteen, I was getting ready for a high school dance, feeling beautiful for once, when my father cornered me, spitting the word "whore" in my face. That was the first time I understood that in my world, love and approval could be withheld at any moment, snatched away like oxygen. It wasn't just fists or insults—it was the constant drumbeat that I didn't matter, that my very existence was offensive. That lesson followed me into adulthood, preparing me for a marriage where the same script played on repeat. That night I pushed back, dared to defend myself, and he punched me, full force in the face. Pain exploded through me. Blood poured as stars burst across my vision, and I ran into the bathroom, locking the door.

When my mother finally came in, I thought maybe, just maybe, she would protect me. Instead, she looked me in the eye and told me it was my fault. That if I were "better," he wouldn't hurt me.

That betrayal cut deeper than the punch.

Desperate for someone to believe me, I reached out to a family member I was close to. But instead of offering help, that family member called my mother to warn her that I needed to keep quiet, that if I didn't, people would "look down on the family." That family member, the one I had trusted my whole life, stood silent. Their loyalty wasn't to the truth. It was to the abuser. Later, these same people would side against me in even bigger ways when the time came to tear me down completely.

By the end of my teenage years, I had learned this lesson: silence was safer than truth. Disappearing was easier than fighting. And that script, hide the hurt, hold the secret, carry the shame, would follow me into adulthood, into relationships, into work, and into the way I saw myself for years to come.

Chapter 8: Learning to Disappear

After those years, something inside me shut down. I stopped expecting safety at home. I stopped expecting my mother to protect me. I stopped expecting family to care. If anything, I learned that family could be just as dangerous as the people who hurt me.

So I disappeared.

On the outside, I was still a teenager, going to school, laughing with friends, and cruising around in cars that smelled like stale French fries and Aqua Net. From a distance, I looked normal.

But inside? I was calculating every move.

Don't say too much. Don't look the wrong way. Don't draw attention. Don't tell anyone the truth.

It was like living with an alarm system wired on high alert. My body went through the motions, but my spirit retreated further and further away. Retreat became my armor. The less of me there was to hurt, the safer I felt.

Of course, disappearing came at a cost. You can't keep shrinking forever without losing something vital. You lose your voice. Your joy. Even the belief that you deserve to take up space.

But at sixteen, I didn't know that yet. All I knew was survival.

That survival script followed me everywhere, into friendships, where I let people use me because speaking up felt dangerous; into relationships, where I confused control with love because silence had been trained into me; into work, where I doubted myself even when I was damn good at what I did.

It took me years, decades, really, to recognize that disappearing wasn't living. Survival mode might keep you alive, but it also keeps you small.

But in those teenage years, disappearing was all I had. And in its own way, it kept me alive long enough to reach the parts of life where I could finally begin reclaiming myself.

Chapter 9: Fighting

Leaving was just the beginning. Survival wasn't about loading a truck and flooring the gas; it was about stepping straight into a war I never signed up for, one I couldn't simply walk away from.

And make no mistake: it was war.

I fought in courtrooms where the scales of justice weren't just tilted, they were bolted to the floor. My ex had the town's golden-boy attorney, the very one who should've been disqualified but wasn't, and a church ready to cast me as the villain. Meanwhile, all I had was me, and whatever scraps of courage I hadn't already burned through.

I filed motions. Appeals. Petitions. I fought tooth and nail for my children, even when I knew the verdict was sealed before I ever walked through the door. My ex played the victim so convincingly that he could have won an Oscar. And behind closed doors, he made sure I knew exactly what role I was assigned: the crazy one, the unfit one, the worthless one. Every whisper, every smirk, every cold shoulder reinforced his message that I didn't matter. It was emotional warfare layered over the physical threats, designed to erase me piece by piece. He'd show up looking pitiful, weaving tales of abuse, while I was cast as the angry, unstable woman who dared to leave.

It was textbook narcissism: projection, manipulation, charm for the audience, cruelty behind the curtain. He didn't even need to be good at it; he just needed an audience willing to believe him. And he had plenty.

The church lined up behind him, eager to offer their "support." My own family, the very people who should have known better, testified against me. They nodded along with the lies. They called me unfit.

Betrayal doesn't even begin to describe it. It felt like being burned alive while the people who shared my blood poured the gasoline.

And still, I fought.

I fought when they stripped me of custody. I fought when they cut off visitation. I fought when the voices around me insisted, again and again, that I was nothing, that I should give up.

There were days I nearly did. Days when depression pressed down like a lead blanket. Days when the silence in my house roared louder than any courtroom. Days when surrender seemed like the only way to stop the ache.

But then I'd see their faces in my mind, my children's laughter, their small hands gripping mine, and I would remember the promise I had made to myself: Every move I make from here on out is for them.

So I fought harder.

I worked jobs that drained me, but I showed up anyway. I stood in courtrooms even when I knew I'd lose, because silence would have meant surrender. I endured the whispers, the gossip, the sideways glances from people who only knew one side of the story. And I carried on with a dignity my abusers never expected me to have.

And maybe the fight wasn't glamorous. I didn't march out of those courtrooms with victories to wave like banners. But survival isn't about looking good on the battlefield; it's about staggering out alive.

And I did.

Every. Damn. Time.

Chapter 10: No One Wins

The brutal truth about divorce and custody battles is that no one wins. Not the husband. Not the wife. And certainly not the children. The only real victors are the lawyers, cashing their checks while you cry yourself to sleep.

By the time the dust settled, I had lost everything that mattered. My children. My family. My church. My reputation. Piece by piece, my entire identity was shredded until there was nothing left of the life I once knew.

The court didn't just rule against me, it erased me. No custody. No visitation. No voice. My ex was handed everything he wanted, and he wielded that power like a weapon. He controlled the narrative. He controlled the children. He controlled the story that everyone else believed.

And me? I was cast as the villain. The unstable mother who "walked away." The problem no one wanted to deal with. The label stuck so tightly that even people who had known me for years began to look at me differently, as if the lies explained everything they thought they saw.

The church clapped from the sidelines, smug in their satisfaction that I had become their cautionary tale, living proof of what happens when a woman refuses to submit. My family cheered too, delighted to see their scapegoat finally nailed to the cross they had built for me decades ago.

And the children? They paid the highest price of all. Kids never win these wars. They were used as pawns, manipulated, lied to, and turned against me. They carried scars I couldn't protect them from. That truth nearly broke me.

I used to lie awake at night, staring at the ceiling, asking myself: What was the point of fighting? I fought until my knuckles bled, until my soul ached, and still I walked away with nothing. Was I a fool for trying? Was it all wasted?

But here's what I've come to understand. Survival doesn't always look like victory. Sometimes survival is crawling across the finish line on your knees, with nothing left but breath. Sometimes survival is being humiliated, betrayed, stripped of everything you love, and still refusing to disappear.

And "still here" meant something.

Because while the court took my children, while the church destroyed my reputation, while my family twisted the knife, none of them got my soul.

That was mine. Untouchable.

So yes, no one wins. But losing everything gave me one thing I had never been offered before: a chance to rebuild from nothing, on my own terms.

And in its own brutal, twisted way, that was a gift.

Chapter 11: Wounds That Follow

People love to say, *"Time heals all wounds."* Cute phrase. Comforting, maybe. But the reality? Some wounds don't heal. They scar. They harden. And they ache when the weather changes.

After the court stripped me of everything, those wounds followed me everywhere. They weren't visible, but they were deafening. Regret has an echo, louder at night when the house is too quiet. Louder when you pass a playground and see mothers pushing their kids on swings. Louder when the phone doesn't ring on your birthday.

There were mornings I couldn't even get out of bed. Depression sat on my chest like a boulder, whispering: What's the point? You've already lost the only people who mattered. And I'll be honest, there were times I thought about letting the dark win. Times when surrender seemed easier than clawing my way through pain that never ended.

The sick twist that checked me every time? The very people who inflicted the wounds were the same ones telling me to "get over it." My family. The church. Even acquaintances who barely knew the story. They acted as if losing your children, your family, and your faith in one crushing blow was something you just bounce back from like a bad haircut.

Meanwhile, I was drowning.

I tried to distract myself with work, with cleaning, with plastering on smiles at the right moments. But the shadow was always there. Some nights I cried until there was nothing left in me. Other nights, I went numb, no tears, no energy, just silence that stretched on forever.

But the worst wound wasn't the abuse. It wasn't even the betrayal. It was the silence from my children. The absence. The hollow where their voices used to be. It felt like living with a phantom limb, you still feel it, you ache for it, but it's gone.

That wound never fully closes.

Wounds are the proof of your battles fought. They remind you that you survived. You can trace them like a map, every scar a mile marker that whispers: You made it through this day. And this one. And this one too.

So I stopped expecting the wounds to disappear. I began to learn to live with them. Some days I wore them like armor. Other days, they crushed me. But slowly, painfully, I began to understand: the wounds would follow me, yes, but they didn't have to define me.

They could haunt me. They could hurt me. But they could never erase me.

Chapter 12: Picking Up the Pieces

At some point, after you've been flattened, broken, and burned to the ground, you realize something: no one is coming to put you back together.

So you start picking up your own damn pieces.

That's where I was. I had lost my children, my family, my church. Everything I thought defined me had been stripped away. Strangely, that emptiness carried its own kind of freedom. When you've been erased, you get to decide who you are from scratch.

The first piece I picked up was me.

For decades, others had told me who I was: the scapegoat, the disappointment, the unstable one, the sinner, the unfit mother. I wore those labels like tattoos I never asked for, inked deep into my skin. But once I was stripped down to nothing, I finally had space to ask the question I'd avoided my whole life: Who am I without their voices in my head?

The answer surprised me.

I wasn't who they said I was. I was someone entirely different.

I began noticing things I'd always pushed aside, flashes of intuition that proved true, dreams that felt more like messages, a quiet knowing that there was more to this world than the punishing God I'd been force-fed. Once the church blinders came off, the universe stretched wide before me, bigger, stranger, and infinitely more beautiful than I had ever been allowed to imagine.

And in that expanse, I discovered something I never expected. I had gifts.

I began to notice things, subtle, undeniable truths about people before they even spoke. I could feel when something was about to happen. Sometimes it came to me in dreams, other times it was just a knowing that settled deep in my bones. And then there was the strangest discovery of all: I could connect with the dead. My old bishop would have branded it demonic. I just called it Tuesday night.

For the first time in my life, spirituality felt expansive instead of suffocating. It wasn't built on guilt or submission. It wasn't about following rules written by men who couldn't even keep their own vows. It was about connection. Energy. Truth.

But picking up the pieces of my life wasn't only spiritual, it was practical too. I worked. I paid bills. I learned to stand on my own two feet. Every independent choice became a quiet victory, proof that I didn't need a man, a church, or even a family to keep me afloat.

It wasn't neat. It wasn't easy. Some days, the pieces felt too jagged, too heavy to lift. Some days, I wanted to crawl back under the covers and disappear. But I didn't. I kept going, one shard at a time, building a new version of myself.

And slowly, something shocking emerged. I hadn't just survived. I was stronger. Sharper. More me than I had ever been.

The pieces didn't fit together the way they once had; they never do. Instead, they formed someone new. Someone authentic. Someone powerful.

Someone free.

Chapter 13: Starting Over

Starting over always sounds glamorous when you read about it in magazines. Fresh chapters. Reinvention. Smiling women in cozy sweaters, sipping lattes.

My version of starting over wasn't glamorous. It was messy. It was terrifying. And it was the most important thing I ever did.

For the first time, I wasn't living for survival or approval. I was living for myself.

And then, against all odds, I met Ken.

Ken wasn't like anyone I'd ever known before. He didn't want to control me. He didn't want to fix me. He didn't need me to shrink so he could shine brighter. He wanted… me. Exactly as I was. Bruises, scars, sharp edges, stubborn streak, sailor's mouth, and all.

At first, I didn't know what to do with that. Trust felt like a foreign language. My default setting was suspicion: What's the catch? When does he turn? When do I have to run?

But he didn't turn. He stayed. He listened. He showed up.

He treated me with a kindness I didn't even know existed. At first, it was unnerving, when you're used to abuse, love feels suspicious. But slowly, I let myself believe it was real.

And it was.

With Ken, I began to rebuild my definition of love. Love wasn't chaos, manipulation, or violence. Love was respect. Love was laughter. Love was someone who had your back, not someone who stabbed it.

Together, we started creating a life. It wasn't perfect, nothing ever is, but it was ours. A home filled with peace instead of screaming. A marriage built on honesty instead of fear. A partnership where both of us mattered.

And in that safe space, I learned something new: how to say no.

No to toxic people. No to manipulative religion. No to guilt that was never mine to carry. No to the voice in my head that still whispered I wasn't enough.

I also discovered my favorite two words: fuck off. I used to be terrified of conflict, having been trained to obey, to shrink, and to apologize for existing. Now? If someone tried to shove me back into that box, I had no problem telling them exactly where they could put it.

Saying no didn't make me hard. It made me softer in the right places. Kinder where it mattered. Because once you stop bleeding energy for people who want to break you, you finally have something left for the people who deserve you.

Ken and I built a life together, not because it was easy, but because it was worth it. Starting over wasn't about erasing the past. It was about refusing to let it define me.

For the first time in my life, I wasn't just surviving.

I was living.

Chapter 14: Death of a Life Once Lived

People love to imagine reconciliation like some Hallmark movie: cue the violins, tears, hugs, and everyone walking hand in hand into a sunset.

That's not how it went for me.

After years of silence and betrayal, my family tried to circle back into my life. Maybe they thought enough time had passed. Maybe they assumed I was desperate enough to rewrite the past. Whatever their reason, they came knocking.

And for a brief moment, I wanted to believe them. I wanted to believe they had changed, that they were finally ready to tell the truth. I wanted to believe we could start fresh. I wanted that Hallmark ending.

Instead, I got a rerun of the same horror show.

The second I let them in, literally and figuratively, the old script followed. The gaslighting. The barbed comments. The sideways digs designed to cut me down. The casual erasure of abuse, as if decades of scars were nothing more than my "overactive imagination."

It felt like stepping back into a play I had already performed, word for word, line for line. Only this time, I refused to play my old role.

The truth was I had changed. My energy, my vibration, my very being no longer matched theirs. I had spent years scraping poison out of my soul, and they were still drinking it for breakfast.

Reuniting didn't feel like healing. It felt like quicksand, pulling me back toward a life I had fought too hard to escape.

So I made a choice. A final one. I let that version of my life die.

The daughter. The sister. The scapegoat.

I buried her. Because she was never allowed to live in their world anyway.

There is grief in that kind of death. Don't let anyone tell you it's easy to cut ties with family. It isn't. It's brutal. It's lonely. It's a wound that reopens every time you see "normal" families laughing together at holidays.

But sometimes death is freedom.

By letting that life die, I stepped fully into the one I was meant to live, one where love was real, not conditional. One where peace was possible, not mocked. One where I finally decided who I was, not them.

And once I closed that door, I locked it.

No more reruns.

No more auditions for their approval.

That life was dead.

And I had no plans to resurrect it.

Chapter 15: Letting Go

"Just let it go."

People toss that phrase around like it belongs on a coffee mug. Easy. Neat. As if all it takes is unclenching your fist, and poof, no more pain.

If only it were that simple.

Letting go isn't one big, cinematic moment. It's a hundred small ones, over and over, where you unclench your jaw, unclench your fists, and stop rehearsing comebacks in the shower for people who aren't even worth the water bill.

For me, letting go meant finally accepting that some people were never going to change—parents, siblings, church leaders, even my ex. They were married to their own version of reality. And in their story, I was always the villain. No amount of explaining, proving, or begging for love could rewrite it. The emotional abuse had trained me to believe I didn't matter, that my worth was conditional, always dangling just out of reach. Letting go meant finally refusing to live inside that lie.

So I stopped auditioning for a role I didn't want.

I let go of my family.

Not in rage. Not in some dramatic explosion. But with clarity. I realized that being related by blood doesn't give someone the right to destroy me. Blood might be thicker than water, but sometimes it's toxic. And I was done drinking poison just because we shared DNA.

I let go of the church.

That was its own kind of freedom. No more bishops deciding if I was "worthy." No more confessions weaponized as gossip. No more pretending God's love came with a 10% price tag. I traded their punishing deity for something bigger, kinder, and far less judgmental: the universe itself.

I let go of guilt.

That one was harder. Guilt had been stitched into my skin since childhood. Every breath, every choice, every misstep felt like proof I was failing someone. But guilt isn't a virtue; it's a chain. And I was exhausted from dragging it behind me like an anchor.

Most of all, I let go of needing to be understood.

That was the hardest release of all. For years, I believed that if I explained myself the right way, eventually someone, my family, my children, or the church, would finally see me clearly. But the truth is, people who don't want to see you never will. And it's not my job to hand out flashlights to people determined to keep their eyes shut.

Letting go didn't mean forgetting. It didn't mean excusing. It meant redirecting all the energy I had wasted on fighting ghosts and pouring it back into myself instead.

And here's what I learned: once you start letting go, you realize how much lighter you feel.

Freedom isn't always about adding more.

Sometimes it's about subtracting what was crushing you all along.

Chapter 16: The Hard Work

People love to romanticize healing. Soft lighting. Yoga poses. Sage smoke curling in the air. Maybe even a latte with a perfect little heart drawn in the foam. Here's the truth: healing isn't pretty. Healing is work. Hard, sweaty, soul-grinding work. The kind where you learn the same lesson a thousand times before it finally sticks. The kind that leaves you wrung out, not glowing.

For me, healing looked like dragging myself out of bed on mornings when depression told me not to bother. It looked like standing in front of the mirror and forcing myself to whisper: You're not crazy. You're not worthless. You're still here.

It looked like therapy sessions where I cried so hard I left dehydrated. Like journaling until my hand cramped. Like sitting in silence with my own thoughts, and, for once, not running from them.

It looked like breaking patterns was welded into me since childhood. And breaking patterns is exhausting. When you've been trained to apologize for existing, it takes Herculean effort to stop saying "sorry" every five seconds. The first time I looked someone in the eye and said no without explaining myself, I braced for lightning to strike.

Spoiler: it didn't.

Healing also meant facing the ugly parts I didn't want to admit lived inside me. The anger. The bitterness. The jealousy of mothers who still had their children. The resentment I carried toward my family. The rage I aimed at the church. For years, I shoved those feelings down like they were radioactive. But repression doesn't neutralize, it ferments. It rots. And it makes you sick.

Letting them out wasn't graceful. It was raw. Loud. Messy. Sometimes it was screaming in my car until my throat burned.

And then there was forgiveness. Not the soft, tidy kind that gets written on greeting cards. Not the "I forgive everyone and send love into the universe" kind. I'm talking about real forgiveness, the kind where you don't excuse what was done to you, but you refuse to carry it. Some people think forgiveness is a gift you give others. I learned it's a gift you give yourself, because holding on to that much rage is like drinking poison and waiting for them to die.

As brutal as the work was, it worked. Slowly. Painfully. Stubbornly. The rubble started to shift. And buried under it, I began to find myself again.

And no, it didn't happen overnight. Healing is not a straight line. Some days, you feel powerful and unstoppable. Other days, you find yourself sobbing in the grocery store because someone called out "Mom," and it wasn't meant for you. Both days count. Both days are part of the work.

The hard work of healing taught me one undeniable truth: you can't shortcut your way to peace.

You have to earn it.

And God knows, I did.

Chapter 17: Ask and You Shall Receive

One of the hardest lessons I ever learned was it's okay to ask.

I grew up believing that asking for anything, love, help, even basic kindness, was a sign of weakness. My family trained me to be grateful for scraps. My marriage taught me that asking was dangerous, because the answer usually came with a fist. The church told me it was fine to ask God, as long as I was ready to accept silence… or blame when nothing changed.

So I didn't ask. I endured. I survived. But I never asked.

It wasn't until I was stripped down to nothing that I realized something revolutionary: the universe wasn't my family. It wasn't my ex. And it sure as hell wasn't the church.

The universe actually responded when I asked.

It started small. I'd whisper, I just need a break today, and something would shift: a smile from a stranger, a bill that didn't show up, a quiet moment I thought I'd never get. Later, I got bolder. I need a job that won't crush me. And opportunities appeared. Not because life had turned magical overnight, but because I finally dared to open my mouth and claim what I needed.

Asking wasn't a weakness. Asking was power.

That doesn't mean I floated off on some cloud of enlightenment. I still doubted. I still cursed. I still cried. But little by little, I learned that when I asked with intention, really asked, the universe listened.

Sometimes it gave me exactly what I wanted. Other times it gave me what I actually needed (annoying, but true). And yes, sometimes the answer was still "not yet." But even then, I began to understand: I wasn't being ignored. I was being prepared.

The trick was surrendering control. You can't ask and then micromanage the outcome like it's a package from Amazon. (Trust me, I tried. The universe does not deliver in two days with free shipping.)

What you can do is ask with clarity, act with intention, and then trust. Trust that what comes is aligned with who you are becoming, not who you used to be.

For me, that changed everything. I had spent a lifetime begging the wrong people to see me, to love me, to treat me like I mattered. The day I stopped begging them and started asking the universe instead, everything shifted.

"Ask and you shall receive" isn't just a cliché. It's a law.

And once I learned that, I never stopped asking.

Chapter 18: Accepting Yourself

For most of my life, I lived under a microscope, and not the flattering kind. Every flaw, every misstep, every emotion was magnified and held up as proof that I was defective. Too sensitive. Too stubborn. Too loud. Too much. Never enough. Always wrong.

After a while, you start to believe it. You begin to see yourself through their warped lens until the only reflection you recognize is the one they painted for you. And let me tell you, it's damn hard to scrub that paint off.

But somewhere between surviving, healing, and learning to trust the universe, I discovered something shocking: I wasn't broken. I wasn't damaged. I wasn't crazy.

I was just me.

And I was enough.

Accepting yourself sounds simple, but it isn't. It's standing in front of a mirror after decades of being told you're worthless and daring to say, I like this person. At first, it felt awkward, like trying on someone else's shoes. But the more I practiced, the more natural it became. Acceptance looked like no longer apologizing for things that weren't my fault. It looked like laughing at my own jokes, even if no one else laughed with me. It looked like trusting my instincts instead of second-guessing every choice because I had been trained to believe I couldn't make good ones.

It also meant embracing the messy parts, the scars, the stubborn streak, the dark humor that sometimes makes people blink twice. For years, those were the traits I'd been punished for. But now, I saw them for what they really were: survival tools. Strengths.

I used to believe acceptance meant finally winning my family's approval, earning the church's stamp of worthiness, or meeting my ex's impossible standards. But I know now the only acceptance that matters is my own.

And let me tell you, that realization is liberating.

There's freedom in saying *Yeah, I'm not perfect. I can be blunt, sarcastic, maybe even intimidating. But I'm also kind, loyal, smart, and strong as hell. Take it or leave it.*

The truth is, I'd rather be hated for who I really am than loved for who I'll never be.

And once I finally accepted myself, I realized something beautiful: I never actually needed their approval.

I only ever needed mine.

Chapter 19: Redemption

Redemption isn't about going back and fixing the past. If it were, I would have marched into that courtroom years ago, slapped the lies out of everyone's mouths, and walked out with my kids to a standing ovation.

But life doesn't hand out do-overs like that.

What I've learned is that redemption is quieter. It's not about proving them wrong. It's about proving yourself right. It's not about rewriting the story they told about you. It's about finally writing your own.

For years, I longed for the cinematic version of redemption, the moment when the people who betrayed me collapsed under the weight of their guilt, begging for forgiveness. Where church leaders who covered up abuse faced real justice. Where my family admitted their lies, manipulation, and cruelty.

Spoiler: that never happened. (And I'm not holding my breath.)

What did happen is that I stopped needing their apologies to feel whole. I stopped waiting for them to see the truth. I stopped handing them the pen for my story.

My redemption came through survival. Through building a life with Ken, rooted in love instead of fear. Through discovering that peace doesn't come from their validation, it comes from my own.

It showed up in the small victories: every time I said no without guilt. Every time I laughed in the face of someone's manipulation. Every time I chose myself over their approval.

And the greatest redemption of all? Still being here.

Because the truth is, they tried to erase me. My parents. My ex. The church. The courts. One after another, they piled on, determined to silence me, to make me disappear.

And yet, here I am. Telling my story. Writing my truth. Refusing to be quiet.

That's redemption.

Not because it erases the pain. Not because it magically restores everything I lost. But because it proves they didn't win.

I'm still standing, stronger, sharper, and more alive than they ever imagined I could be.

And that? That's enough.

Chapter 20: Letting Go of That Which Does Not Serve You

If I've learned anything on this journey, it's that not everything, or everyone, deserves a seat at your table.

For years, I let people and institutions feed off me like parasites. My family drained me with their judgment. My ex drained me with his abuse. The church drained me with guilt and shame. I was starving, and they still wanted seconds.

At some point, you have to cut the cord.

Letting go of what doesn't serve you isn't selfish; it's survival. It's drawing a line in the sand and saying: If it costs me my peace, it's too expensive.

So I started dropping the dead weight.

First, the toxic people. The ones who smiled in public but stabbed me in private. The family who gaslit me. The friends who betrayed me. The so-called leaders who hid behind titles while enabling abuse. Gone. They didn't get explanations. They didn't get drawn-out goodbye speeches. They just got cut, like diseased branches trimmed from a tree.

Then, the beliefs. The lie that I had to earn love. The idea that my worth depended on obedience. The poison that suffering made me holy. Straight to the curb.

And maybe most importantly, I let go of the version of myself who bent over backward trying to prove she was enough. She worked hard.

She kept me alive. But she was exhausted, broken, and always begging for scraps. I honored her, and then I released her.

Here's the beautiful part: when you let go of what doesn't serve you, you make space for what does.

Real love. Real joy. Real peace. Things I didn't even know were possible while I was carrying all that junk.

It's like cleaning out a closet. At first, you hesitate. But what if I need this later? you think, clutching a sweater you haven't worn in fifteen years. But once you toss it, you realize it was only taking up space. The same goes for toxic people, false beliefs, and outdated versions of yourself.

Letting go doesn't mean forgetting. It doesn't mean excusing. It means refusing to let poison drip into your life one more day

I used to think holding on made me strong.

Now I know: real strength is letting go.

And nothing feels more powerful than looking at something or someone who once had control over you and saying, 'No more.'

Chapter 21: Telling Them All to F*** Off

By this point in my life, I had mastered a new skill: the art of saying fuck off.

And I don't mean stomping around, screaming it at every barista who forgets the oat milk. I mean something deeper. A soul-level declaration that I was done letting people, or institutions, control me, define me, or drain me.

For years, I swallowed my words. I was trained to. Good daughters stayed quiet. Good wives obeyed. Good church members submitted. Every time I bit my tongue, every time I shrank to fit someone else's narrative, a little piece of me died.

Well, that girl is gone. In her place stands a woman who isn't afraid to say it straight: fuck off.

To my abusive ex: fuck off. You tried to break me, erase me, destroy me. And yet, here I am, stronger, louder, and happier than you ever thought possible. You didn't win.

To my family: fuck off. You wanted a scapegoat, someone to carry your shame so you wouldn't have to face it yourselves. You picked me. But I'm not carrying it anymore. That's your baggage. Pack it yourself.

To the church: fuck off. You covered up abuse, protected predators, and shamed survivors. You told me I was broken when I was whole all along. You will never again get to tell me who I am, what I'm worth, or how I connect to God.

And to guilt, shame, and fear, the three-headed monsters that stalked me most of my life: fuck right off. You don't live here anymore.

Telling people to fuck off isn't about rage. It's about boundaries. It's about reclaiming the space in your life that belongs to you. It's about realizing your worth isn't up for debate, and you don't owe explanations to anyone who refuses to see it.

The first time I said it out loud, I laughed. It felt so good, like yanking out a splinter that had been festering for decades. The more I said it, the easier it became. Not always out loud, sometimes it was just a quiet fuck off in my head when someone tried to shove me back into the box. Either way, it worked.

And let me tell you, once you master the art of fuck off, your life changes. You stop chasing people who don't deserve you. You stop apologizing for things that aren't your fault. You stop tolerating bullshit disguised as "love," "faith," or "family."

You finally, fully, unapologetically become yourself.

And if someone can't handle that?

Well… they already know the answer.

Chapter 22: Bumps in the Road

No one tells you that healing doesn't make life perfect. You don't graduate with a shiny diploma that says, Congratulations, you're healed! From here on out, it's smooth sailing.

Nope. Life keeps life-ing.

Even after all the work, all the letting go, all the boundaries, all the fuck offs, the universe still throws bumps in the road. Unexpected bills. Health scares. Arguments. Loss. Some days you feel unstoppable, and the next you're crying in the grocery store because a song on the loudspeaker guts you out of nowhere.

The difference now is in how I handle the bumps.

Before, every setback felt like proof I was broken. Every challenge was evidence that my family, my ex, and the church were right about me all along. I'd spiral into shame, convinced I was failing again.

Now? I see bumps for what they are: part of the road, not the end of it.

When something hard shows up, I don't collapse like I used to. I pause. I breathe. Sometimes I cuss a little (okay, a lot). Then I remind myself: You've been through worse and survived. You can handle this, too.

And it's true. After you've lived through violence, betrayal, and losing your children, a flat tire or a bad day at work doesn't exactly take you down. Even the big things, grief, disappointment, heartbreak, they still hurt, but they don't erase me anymore.

I've also learned to laugh at the bumps. Humor is its own kind of survival. Like the time I tripped over my own rug and landed flat on my back. Ten years ago, I would've cursed myself for being "clumsy and stupid." Now? I laughed so hard I cried, then texted Ken that the rug was clearly possessed.

The bumps don't define me anymore. They remind me I'm human. They keep me humble. They keep me grateful for the fact that I'm still here to feel them at all.

Life isn't perfect. Healing doesn't erase the mess. But the mess doesn't scare me anymore.

I can handle the bumps.

Hell, sometimes I even enjoy the ride.

Chapter 23: Life Is Not Perfect

I wish I could tell you that after all the healing, all the letting go, all the fuck offs, I stepped into a flawless life where everything finally clicked into place.

But that would be a lie.

Life is not perfect. Healing doesn't erase triggers, old wounds, or the voices that still whisper doubt at the worst possible times. I still get tangled in my thoughts. I still overthink. I still replay the old tapes from people who never deserved space in my memory in the first place.

The difference now is simple. I don't live there anymore.

And one of the biggest reasons for that is Ken.

Ken isn't perfect, thank goodness. Perfect people don't exist, and if they did, they'd be insufferable. But he is perfect for me.

When I start spinning in my head, he steadies me. When I forget how far I've come, he reminds me. When I slip back into old patterns of guilt or self-doubt, he calls me out, not with cruelty, not with judgment, but with a steady love that says, 'I see you.' You're safe. Come back to yourself.

He has been my counselor, my cheerleader, my safe place to land. He listens when I need to rant. He holds me when I need to cry. Sometimes, he simply sits beside me in silence when there aren't any words.

And the best part? He has never seen me as broken. From the very beginning, he recognized strength in me that I couldn't yet see in myself. He didn't love me despite my scars; he loved me with them.

That doesn't mean it's always easy. Marriage takes work, even the good kind. We disagree. We frustrate each other. He drives me crazy sometimes, and I'm sure I return the favor. But the difference is this- we fight with each other, not against each other. We fight for the relationship, not to win the argument.

And after everything I've lived through, that feels like a miracle.

So no, life isn't perfect. But it's real. It's honest. It's grounded in love, respect, and laughter. And after the chaos I came from, that feels like the best kind of perfection.

Ken may not be flawless. Neither am I. But together, we are exactly what we need to be: whole.

Chapter 24: Stand Your Ground

One of the hardest and most important lessons I've learned is how to stand my ground. It's a skill that has saved me more times than I can count.

For most of my life, I didn't. I bent. I folded. I gave in. I kept quiet. I believed love meant sacrificing myself, and survival meant keeping everyone else happy. But every time I surrendered my ground, I lost another piece of myself.

Not anymore.

Now, I know exactly where I stand. And I don't move just because someone else is uncomfortable with it. My boundaries are not negotiable. My voice is not up for debate. My peace is not for sale.

Here's the beauty of it- standing your ground doesn't mean standing alone.

I have Ken beside me. And he's not just my partner, he's my backup, my anchor, and often the comic relief that keeps life bearable. His sense of humor is unmatched. We laugh every single day, often at the small absurdities that used to weigh me down. That laughter isn't just fun; it's medicine. It's proof that joy can exist even after everything.

Do we disagree? Of course. Sometimes we argue. But those moments don't weaken us; they strengthen us. Because every disagreement is grounded in respect. He never belittles me. I never have to shrink myself for him. We work through it. We grow stronger.

Ken is kind. He is steady, the kind of steady you can lean on when the world feels unsteady. He doesn't punish me for being human. He meets me where I am and stays with me there.

That's why standing my ground has become possible. Because when you know who you are and have someone who loves you exactly as you are, you stop apologizing for existing.

Standing your ground isn't about anger or hardness. It's about knowing your worth, refusing to settle for less, and surrounding yourself with people who build you instead of breaking you down.

Ken and I have built a life where laughter and love are the foundation, and respect is the rule. That's what makes us strong. That's what makes me strong.

So yes, life still throws challenges. Yes, people still try to cross my lines. But now, I don't flinch. I don't fold. I stand my ground, smiling, laughing, and sometimes cracking a sarcastic joke while I do it.

Because strength doesn't always need to roar. Sometimes, strength looks like love. Sometimes, it looks like laughter.

And sometimes, it looks like standing your ground with someone who will always stand beside you.

Chapter 25: Integrity (Your Pillar)

If there's one thing I've fought tooth and nail to protect, it's my integrity.

When everything else was stripped away, my reputation, my family's approval, even my children, I still had one thing no one could touch: my truth.

People lied about me. They twisted stories. They painted me as the villain because it was easier than facing the reality of abuse, dysfunction, and hypocrisy. But through it all, I refused to let their lies become my truth. I refused to play their game.

Integrity became my anchor.

It meant speaking the truth, even when my voice trembled. It meant holding myself accountable, even when others refused to do the same. It meant choosing authenticity over acceptance, peace over popularity.

I can live without a lot of things. But I cannot live without integrity. Because at the end of the day, when I look in the mirror, I want to recognize the woman staring back.

That's the legacy I want to leave behind, not the abuse I endured, not the betrayals I survived, but the strength of knowing I never lost myself in the process.

And most importantly, that's the legacy I want my children to see.

Even if they don't believe me yet.

Even if their hearts and minds are clouded by lies and manipulation.

Even if they can't see me clearly today.

Someday, they will.

Because integrity outlasts everything else. Lies eventually collapse. Masks eventually fall. But truth? It endures.

And when my children look back, when they start searching for what was real and what was fabricated, I want them to find a mother who, no matter what, stood tall in her truth.

That's why I write this. That's why I speak it. That's why I keep going, even when the ache of their absence nearly breaks me.

Integrity isn't just my pillar.

It's my promise.

It's my love letter to them.

Chapter 26: To My Children

My loves, this chapter is for you.

I know that for much of your lives, you've only heard one version of who I am. And I know that version hasn't been kind. You've been told stories that portrayed me as the villain, the problem, the failure, the one who was never enough. Those stories were easier to believe than facing the truth about the people and systems that hurt us all.

But I want you to know this: I have always loved you. From the very first moment I held each of you, I was forever changed. My love for you has never wavered, not in the darkest courtrooms, not in the loneliest nights, not in the silence that has stretched painfully between us.

Yes, I made mistakes. I am not a perfect mother, no one is. But I was never the monster they made me out to be. I was a young woman, scared and broken, doing her best inside a marriage and a religion that tried to crush her spirit. I fought battles you never saw, often alone, and sometimes I lost. But I never stopped fighting for myself. And I never stopped loving you.

The day I lost you, not because I let go, but because lies and power convinced the world that I was unfit, was the day my heart shattered. And yet, even in that loss, I chose to keep going. Not because it was easy, but because I knew if I gave up, then their version of me would win.

And I wanted you to grow up and someday find me still standing.

So here I am.

Still standing. Still loving you. Still hoping that one day you'll see me clearly, not through the lens of gossip, not through the church's judgment, not through the lies that were told about me, but through your own eyes.

You may not understand right now. You may not want to. And that's okay. This book isn't written to force you into my arms. It's here to give you my truth. To put on record the life I lived, the battles I fought, and the love that carried me through every single storm.

You are my greatest heartbreak and my greatest hope.

No matter how much time passes, no matter what you've been told, you will always be my children. I will always be here. My arms will always be open.

Not with strings. Not with demands. Just with love.

Because at the end of it all, that's who I am. That's what I have to give. And that will never change.

I love you.

I always have.

I always will.

Mom

Chapter 27: Closing Words

Thank you for reading my words.

This isn't the story I thought I'd be telling when I was nineteen, standing in a white dress at the altar, convinced that obedience would keep me safe. It isn't the story I thought I'd be telling in a courtroom, losing what mattered most to me. And it certainly isn't the story I thought I'd be telling in the darkness of night, when I wondered if my life had already been decided for me.

But it is the story I needed to tell.

Life doesn't hand out fairytales. It hands out heartbreak. Lies. Betrayal. People who will swear you're something you're not. It hands out bumps in the road, sometimes gaping potholes that you stumble into headfirst.

But life also hands out second chances. Laughter. Sunrises. Unexpected kindness. The strength to stand up one more time after being knocked flat.

And that's what I want you to carry with you, whether you are my children, a stranger holding this book, or someone quietly fighting battles no one else can see. Healing isn't about erasing the scars. It's about learning to live with them. To laugh with them. To even love them.

You don't have to be perfect to be worthy. You don't have to have it all figured out to begin again. And you don't owe your worth to anyone unwilling to see it.

Stand your ground. Protect your integrity. Laugh often (sarcasm highly recommended). And when life knocks you down, don't just get back up; get back up swinging, laughing, or dancing, whichever feels right that day.

Because you can rise. You can heal. You can build a life that feels like your own, no matter where you came from or what was taken from you.

This isn't the end of my story. And it isn't the end of yours either.

It's simply the reminder that even when life isn't perfect, it can still be breathtakingly beautiful.

And that, scars, laughter, love, and all, is enough.

-Katie

www.ingramcontent.com/pod-product-compliance
Lightning Source LLC
Chambersburg PA
CBHW070351130626
46556CB00007B/3133